Northern Alchemy

Northern Alchemy

CHRISTINE DE LUCA

PATRICIAN PRESS
MANNINGTREE

First published as a paperback edition by Patrician Press 2020

British Library Cataloguing in Publication Data. A catalogue record for this book is available from the British Library.

ISBN paperback edition 978-1-9997030-8-0

Published by Patrician Press 2020

Christine De Luca *lives in Edinburgh. She writes in English and Shetlandic, her mother tongue. She was appointed Edinburgh's Makar (poet laureate) for 2014-2017. Besides several children's stories (in Shetlandic) and one novel, she has had seven poetry collections and four bi-lingual volumes published (French, Italian, Icelandic and Norwegian) and has been active in translation. She has also co-authored/ edited two books including her poems, most recently Paolozzi at Large in Edinburgh (Luath Press, 2018).*

Website including audio files:
www.christinedeluca.co.uk

Foreword

'Raised wi twa languages
is unconscious faestin: twa wyes o tinkin.'

from Sam but different

Christine De Luca has achieved what Shetland writers
in former times would have considered impossible: her
writing in her beloved native tongue is known and
admired both at home and outwith the islands. In
Shetland, it used to be accepted that writing in
Shetlandic would be of little or no interest to most of
the outside world. Christine has happily defied such
predictions. From the beginning, she wrote in both
English and in Shetland dialect, and was gratified to
discover how well the dialect was received by listeners
and readers. It was and is at the core of her identity,
and she revels in it. Her poetry, and her own readings
of it, has brought the real sound of Shetland to a
national and international audience.

Her work, while deeply rooted in the islands, is
wide-ranging, regularly encompassing new thoughts
and topics. She delights in the natural world, and in the
joys of life, while fully aware of its transience and its
darker sides. Her enthusiasm for words and language
never dims, nor does her dialect voice. Selections of her
poems have been translated into Italian, French,

Norwegian and Icelandic; it is a joy now to see this parallel Shetland – English selection, spanning the time-frame and spectrum of her writing career.

This collection, above all, should promote understanding of the dialect which means so much to Christine De Luca. She proves time and time again how her native tongue is worth using, worth delving into, worth loving for its potential for description, for flow, for precision of meaning. In skilled hands like her own, it brings images and thoughts to vibrant life, turns phrases into music, and can 'greet and sing' at the same time.

To the young, to the curious, to the newcomer to Shetland speech, to its native speakers, its admirers, detractors, and those who may never have seriously considered it as a medium for poetry – this book is for you all. Read, understand, enjoy!

Laureen Johnson

Co-editor, The New Shetlander

Contents

Introduction

Until relatively recently it was almost impossible to have a poetry collection with other than a *soupçon* of poems in Shetlandic published in the mainstream, particularly by the better known, largely metropolitan publishers. It was even difficult to have such work published on the mainland of Scotland. The choices available for Shetland poets were therefore: to be published only locally; to have a negligible proportion of dialect poems in a collection; to write in English (with perhaps a tiny smattering of Shetland vocabulary) or – as prose writers have found – to water down the linguistic richness of the dialect to make it easier to read. For me, I could only live with the first of these options. Anything else felt like selling-out.

Indigenous 'mother tongue' is, by its very nature, a response to its physical and cultural environment. Not only do I write from a need to express thought and feeling using the full-bodied dialect (even if sometimes that makes it a little difficult for the reader) but also, given that Shetlandic, like so many minority tongues, faces extinction if not used, it is hard to sidestep a sense of stewardship. Hence I embrace the challenging – and possibly linguistically controversial – proposition that 'language is a dialect with a literature'. In some ways the EU, despite its dominant languages, has enabled minority tongues to be heard and supported and this has perhaps encouraged more interest in, and recently a fashion for, publishing work with a feeling of liminality, periphery or linguistic or cultural distinctiveness. However, it is still a brave publisher who takes this on.

So what is Shetlandic or Shetland dialect (I tend to use the words interchangeably)? Given that Shetland was part of the Danish-Norwegian kingdom until the late 15th century – becoming Scottish as part of a dowry pledge of the Danish princess – the original language was Norn, one of the Scandinavian family of languages. Gradually the islands came under the influence of Scotland and the Scots tongue. Norn was no longer the language of power and was pushed to the margins. However, much of the sound quality and vocabulary still remain even today, making the Shetland tongue a distinctive hybrid related both to Old Scots and its Nordic roots. Scandinavian writers with whom I'm in contact tend to describe it as a 'cousin' language, and understand it as much from their own languages as from English which they all speak with enviable fluency.

I have been fortunate to have found an interest in Shetlandic on the continent for several years now, expressed in a willingness of editors and publishers not only to translate my poems but also to publish bi-lingual editions. And not only in Icelandic and Norwegian but also in French and Italian. An Icelandic translator/ editor/ publisher, Aðalsteinn Ásberg Sigurdsson, also produced a contemporary bi-lingual Shetland poetry anthology, Hjaltlandsljóð, which was a first and much appreciated by Shetland poets. (Dimma, Reykjavik, 2012)

However, at last – a bi-lingual in English! I am delighted that Patrician Press is willing to publish this book. The poems are arranged chronologically, rather than thematically. I have happily provided the English versions of the poems. My intention in creating these English versions is to give as accurate a translation as possible, rather than compromise for the sake of making it 'poetic' in English or hiding behind the idea that it is somehow untranslatable, tempting though that may be. There are, however, many words without appropriate English equivalents (see notes), as exemplified in the poem Yarbent (page 36). Many English speakers find that they can sound the poems out phonetically and that, when they hear the poems read, they are not so unfamiliar.

Christine De Luca
August, 2019

Shetlandic poems with English versions

The Shetlandic poems and the English versions appear side by side. When the Shetlandic poem consists of two pages, then it is shown in its entirety, as is the English version, rather than each page appearing opposite each other. The text in the English versions is in grey.

Gyaain ta da eela

Vaila darkenin fae aest ta wast,
wind faa'n awa;
eela nichts i da simmer dim.

Abön da tide, laek a sel, wir boat wid lie;
we hed ta tize her doon,
bulderin an traan owre da ebb
but nyiff i da sea.

Rowin oot bi wir kent wirld
ta da uncan moo o da Waster Soond,
holms lay black on a sea an sky o gowld.

We'd row til da holm o Burrastow cam clos
dan drap da dorro;
een o wis wid aandoo, boos ta da wind.

Waands owre da starn,
piltocks nyggin:
up dey'd come wi a bummel,
sheenin, spricklin,
dan prammed an pechin at wir fit.

Lines unreffelled
owre da side again
roond an roond da skerry
waatchin fur froad braakin on da baas.
Gleg een, quick haands;
piltocks takkin
bucket fillin
ee mair time
maybe twa.
Dan aathin quiet an da hömin closin in.

Packin up wir proil, we'd mak fur haem,
blyde o kent lichts. We'd row
peerie-wyes, owsin as we göd.
Abön wis, tirricks flitin
an a mird o maas laavin an divin,
plötin fur muggies.

We'd tak da boat in on a flowin tide,
dicht an shoard her, dan rin haem prood
i da darkenin wi a fraacht o fysh.

We'd aet wir supper
tae tales o uncan Odysseys
in idder voes.

Going evening sea-fishing

Vaila darkening from east to west,
wind easing;
fishing in the long light of summer evenings.

Above the tideline, like a seal, our boat would lie;
we had to tempt her down,
blundering clumsily, awkward over the foreshore
but nimble in the sea.

Rowing out beyond our known world
to the unfamiliar mouth of the Western Sound,
holms lay black on a sea and sky of gold.

We'd row until the holm of Burrastow came close
then drop the weighted hand-line;
one of us would row gently, bows into the wind.

Fishing rods over the stern,
saithe tugging:
up they'd come with a floundering,
shining, wriggling,
then packed in and gasping at our feet.

Lines untangled
over the side again
round and roond the skerry
watching for foam breaking on the submerged rocks.
Alert eyes, quick hands;
saithe taking
bucket filling
one more time
maybe two.
Then everything quiet and the twilight closing in.

Packing up our booty, we'd set off for home,
glad of familiar lights. We'd row
gently, baling as we went.
Above us, arctic terns scolding angrily
and a throng of seagulls hovering and diving,
pleading for fish-guts.

We'd take the boat in on a flowing tide,
tidy and prop her up, then run home proud
in the darkening with a burden of fish.

We'd eat our supper
to tales of strange Odysseys
in other *voes*.

Gyaain fur da mylk

Da shortest gaet ta Bardister
wis up da daal, makkin a trenkie
trowe unma'an girse,
round bi da lochside
an toons o Kurkigert;
on bi da paety hols
atween da lochs – but no owre near
fur fock said you'd laand *doon under*
if you weet your feet –
owre Vatnabrug, a muckle slab
across da burn, smoothed
trowe centuries
bi trows an traivellers.
Hit wis wir Rubicon in simmer:
nae shunner crossed
dan tirrick squadrons scrambled
ta warn wis aff der nests.
We'd rin, pel flailin owre wir heads
ta hadd dem aff,
spangin stanks o yallow blugga
shastit bi da caald clos pirr o wings.
At last, da nae man's laand o Bardister,
an der retreat. Waarm whalps
wid rin ta meet wis:
a thoosand licks, an aa wir faer
o haemward baff
wis gien.

Anidder simmer gaet wis owre da hill;
anidder wirld: wild open heogan,
moss an hedder-kowes,
berries, sookies, drummie-bees –

– sookies gied a snyirk
whin pooed, an cam clean oot;
wan flooer, wan honeyed sook,
primeval gadderin –
Whaaps an peewits keepit watch;
dey nivver möved but passed
der warnin cries aroond.
Nests wis denkies i da grund
wi eggs or bruckit shalls.

At last, leg weary, we'd come apö
da hill-grind, twa hooses
an da rigs o Bardister.

Pels lined da porch,
some wi blaand or bleddick
sharp-smelled an snyipperin;
fur wis, sweet mylk
still waarm.

We'd mak fur haem, pel daddin,
unawaar o foo a kirn o memory
wid turn sae lang
an still sustain.

Fetching the milk

The shortest path to Bardister
was up the valley, making a passage
through unmown grass,
round by the lakeside
and fields of Kirkigarth;
on past the peaty hollows
between the lakes – but not too near
for folk said you'd land *down under*
if you wet your feet –
over Vatnabrug: a massive slab
across the stream, smoothed
through centuries
by trolls and walkers.
It was our Rubicon in summer:
no sooner crossed
than tern squadrons scrambled
to warn us off their nests.
We'd run, pail flailing overhead
to hold them off,
leaping ditches of marsh-marigold
chased by the cold close draught of wings.
At last, the no-man's land of Bardister,
and their retreat. Warm pups
would run to meet us;
a thousand licks, and all our fear
of homeward tussle
was gone.

Another summer path was over the hill;
another world: wild open common,
moss and bushy heather,
berries, lousewort, bumble-bees

– lousewort gave a squeak
when pulled, and came clean out;
one flower, one honeyed suck,
primeval gathering –
Curlew and lapwing kept watch;
they never moved but passed
their warning cries around.
Nests were hollows in the ground
with eggs or broken shells.

At last, leg-weary, we'd reach
the hill-gate, two houses
and the fields of Bardister.

Pails lined the porch,
some with whey or buttermilk
sharp-smelled and puckering;
for us, fresh milk
still warm.

We'd set off for home, pail thumping,
unaware of how a churn of memory
would turn so long
and still sustain.

Queer things, smiles

A baby's smile
is a hale boady affair:
a pooster o airms an legs
seekin ta plaese.

A bairn's smile
wirks on wis, kyöderin
till we gie in.

A blinnd man's smile
is nae less fur hits eelessness:
laerned ithoot seein
foo a smile bracks.

Da smile o a uncan boady,
– a blate risk o a kennin
we geng da sam gaet –
bals jöst enyoch caution
tae da wind.

Da smile o a loved wan
– dat peeriest glink i da een at says
mair as we dare tink true –
caa's owre an biggs
at een an da sam time;
hit maks a bassel o pairtin.

Strange things, smiles

A baby's smile
is a whole body affair:
an energy of arms and legs
wanting to please.

A child's smile
works on us, ingratiating
till we give in.

A blind man's smile
is no less for its eyelessness:
learned without seeing
how a smile breaks.

The smile of a stranger,
– a shy risk of a knowing
we travel the same road –
throws just enough caution
to the wind.

The smile of a loved one
– that tiniest gleam in the eye that says
more than we dare think true –
knocks down and builds
at one and the same time;
it makes a struggle of parting.

Wan wirld at Bluemull Soond

Linga bracks da Bluemull Soound
smooth as a neesick.
Tirricks lift fae ferry furrows,
sweep backwards in circles
skoitin fur sillocks: dey dive
an rise in perfect verticals.
Anidder ferry comes an still dey laav:
whit strug fur sic a peerie paek.

Alang da banks
a swaabie tips an penks
traepin fur maet.
Tief at he is, he shastes dem
till dey drap der catch.

He'll no fant
nor yet his kind
while peerie tirricks fish
da Bluemull Soound.

One world at Bluemull Sound

Linga breaks the Bluemull Sound
smooth as a porpoise.
Arctic terns lift from ferry furrows,
sweep backwards in circles
peering for saithe: they dive
and rise in perfect verticals.
Another ferry comes and still they hover:
what toil for such a morsel.

Along the cliffs
a great black-backed gull is jaunty, showing off
nagging for food.
Thief that he is, he chases them
till they drop their catch.

He'll not go hungry
nor yet his kind
while little terns fish
the Bluemull Sound.

Wast wi da Valkyries

Dark burn ta voe, a rinkel
bi Nederdale, trist slow slockit
in a sea-baaled ayre. At da beach
o Dale, noosts gaan at Foula, turn
vod een ta her shaalds. Fae Muness
shö's held in a artist's haand:
Valhalla, veiled paradise, built
laek a saga ta swall ta her heichts
wi every seein, every tellin. Winjanes
means whit hit's aye meant:
headland fur pasture. Ponies
startle dere, tak ta da hill.
Der manes lift laek a dizzen Valkyries
fleein da battle. Laand an sea
is still a skirmish. Unawaar,
selkies rowl i da laebrack,
bask safely on Sel Ayre.
An kittiwaegs cruise, effortless
rollerbladers o da banks.
Da erne at eence ruled dem
is lang gien fae his stack.

Ivery sea bicht riven
fae Dale ta Deebdaal
has jaws risped wi yackles.
Time is mizzered here
bi da sea's favours: a tirse
o takkin, grindin,
a endless beachin; but fur wis,
travaillers o da wastern aedge,
hit's a time ta tak, ta pick owre

gaets wir taen, or no taen,
on dis wir langest vaege.

West with the Valkyries

Dark stream to *voe*, a tinkle
past Netherdale, thirst slowly slaked
in a sea-thrown barrier. At the beach
of Dale, *noosts* gaze at Foula, turn
empty eyes to her fishing shallows. From Muness
she's held in an artist's hand:
Valhalla, veiled paradise, built
like a saga to swell to her heights
with every seeing, every telling. Winjanes
means what it has always meant:
headland for pasture. Ponies
startle there, dash up the hill.
Their manes lift like a dozen Valkyries
fleeing the battle. Land and sea
are still a skirmish. Unaware,
seals roll in the breaking surf,
bask safely on Sel Ayre.
And kittiwakes cruise, effortless
roller-bladers of the cliffs.
The sea-eagle that once ruled them
is long gone from his rocky sea-stack.

Every sea inlet torn
from Dale to Deep Dale
has jaws sharp with molars.
Time is measured here
by the sea's favours: a temper
of taking, grinding,
an endless depositing; but for us,
walkers of the western edge,
it's a time to take, to pick over

paths we have taken, or not taken,
on this our longest journey.

Lizzie Coutts' Knowe

Oot o scöl on winter days, we'd sprit
across da fud ta Lizzie Coutts' Knowe
sledges nyiggin at wir heels laek aaber whalps.

Hills wirna better med fur sledgin:
low enyoch fur a quick bassel tae da tap;
steep enyoch ta taste da aedge
o danger; lang enyoch ta savour.

We'd pile on
twartree o wis
een on tap o tidder:
belly-gutsie fur da brave
nae trace o faer.
Da runk o iron apö ice,
snaa spindrifts smookin
i da face. A rummel
o scriechs as we swooshed
owre every bump
afore we cummelled.

Dan haem fur tae, glivs ice-mattit,
haands red raw wi pooin apö kiarr.
Inbye fae da spunder o da nicht
wi haet tiftin anunder wir nails
an wir een blinndit i da licht.

Lizzie Coutts' Hill

Out of school on winter days, we'd race
across the *fud* to Lizzie Coutts' Hill
sledges tugging at our heels like eager pups.

No hill was better for sledging:
low enough for a quick struggle to the top;
steep enough to taste the edge
of danger; long enough to savour.

We'd pile on
two or three of us
one on top of t'other:
face-downwards for the brave
no trace of fear.
Resounding rhythms of iron upon ice,
a gasp of snow spray catching
in the face. A collapse
in screeching as we swished
o'er every bump
before we toppled.

Then home for tea, gloves ice-matted,
hands red-raw with pulling on coir rope.
Inside from the racing of the night
with heat throbbing under our nails
and our eyes blinded in the light.

Da cockle shall

Bousta, Sannis

Gyo o Bousta, roond as a cockle: we'd watch
fur sels here, skyip steyns, kyemp fur da finest shalls.
We'd barely lift wir een ta see hits shape:
dat sam shall pattren at spread hitsel
owre midders' makkin: therteen loops taen in
dan löt oot slowly on a oppenwark o gengs:
waves at shadit ta inky-blueness wi da wind.

Daday, ooers swittle trowe dy fingers
as du seeks, as eence I sowt, da perfect steyn
ta skyip. Tree skyips 'll dö, een mair as last year.
Da rings du maks spread fast. Last simmer here
eicht selkies bobbit laek bowes: eyed wis, dived,
eyed wis again. Dey left nae spreadin rings:
art hoidin artistry. I watch dy steyn dance,

defy da wyes o watter, da skyip o years.
Wi dee A'm richt back: we skile fur sels,
seek cockle shalls, weigh da import o steyns;
skyip an höve dem, fur da sea ta bring back,
ta lay up and mak again in time's lap.

The cockle shell

Bousta, Sannis

Gyo of Bousta, round as a cockle: we'd watch
for seals here, skip stones, compete for finest shells.
We'd barely lift our eyes to see its shape:
that same shell pattern that spread itself
over mothers' knitting: thirteen stitches taken in
then let out slowly over rows of lace:
waves that shaded to inky-blueness with the wind.

Today, hours splash gently through your fingers
as you seek, as once I sought, the perfect stone
to skip. Three skips will do, one more than last year.
The rings you make spread fast. Last summer here
eight seals bobbed like net floats: eyed us, dived,
eyed us again. They left no spreading rings:
art hiding artistry. I watch your stone dance,

defy the ways of water, the skip of years.
With you I'm right back: we search for seals,
seek cockle shells, weigh the import of stones;
skip and throw them, for the sea to bring back,
to cast on and knit again in time's lap.

Hairst mön owre Hjøllund

Denmark

A hairst mön raise apö seed gadderers as dey purled
late ita saandy aert, willin wild girse ta growe tick.
Awaar o dem fae da forest, deer smootit inta mirknen.

Laek a hyook, shö hung high, as fock traipsed haem
clugs truckin rigs o stubble, laevin laand trig stookit.
Deer fled da scent o hirdin, an bere in wippit baands.

Whin da first horses booed tae da bend, a man wid set
da reaper's basque: maa da sweerie-geng. While deer
tippit tae a filsket mön, horses strained i der stall.

Dastreen, shö kyempit wi lichts fae a combine at glaepit
ten fit swaars at ee sitten. Twa deer shivered trowe da bere,
makkin hit ring as dey reeselled da hingin heads.

Harvest moon over Hjøllund

Denmark

A harvest moon rose over seed-gatherers as they groped
late in the sandy earth, willing wild grass to grow thick.
Aware of them from the forest, deer slunk into twilight.

Like a sickle, she hung high, as folk wandered home
clogs trampling fields of stubble, leaving land neatly stacked.
Deer fled the scent of harvest, barley in twisted bands.

When the first horses bowed to the harness, a man would set
the reaper's basque, mow the outer row. While deer
danced to a playful moon, horses strained in their stall.

Last night, she competed with lights from a combine that gulped
three metre swathes at one sitting. Two deer shivered through
barley, making it ring as they shook the hanging heads.

Starn sign

Vidlin 21.10.1914

Nor haeven nor aert is bön at paece da nicht.
War's runnicks barely cut, still lines on maps.
But life gengs on: a ting o lass is boarn.

Birth's bassel owre, da howdie maks fur haem
doon da toons o Neegirt, wi tengs o fire fur licht.
An i da firmament, a comet's flicht records
da moment, ootstrips a hairst mön as shö rides
da sky. Da haevens demsels blaze furt nativity,
hap a blissin on a peerie ting whase first braeth
reincarnates da stoor o galaxies, obscures,
reveals: links daeth wi life an love an po'er.

Star sign

Vidlin 21.10.1914

Nor heaven nor earth has been at peace tonight.
War's trenches barely cut, still lines on maps.
But life goes on: a little girl is born.

Birth's struggle done, the midwife sets off home
down Neegirt's fields, with lit peat held for light.
And in the firmament, a comet's flight records
the moment, outstrips a harvest moon that rides
the sky. The heavens themselves blaze forth nativity,
wrap a blessing round a little one whose first breath
reincarnates the dust of galaxies, obscures,
reveals: links death with life and love and power.

Bio-rhythms

Fur as lang as sea is töllied wi da laand
an maalies sowt a skelf ita da banks
der haerse cackle is bön a haemward hymn
a warnin cry. Wan at sea, wan on da nest
een spellin tidder: comins an gyaains mapped
bi a swaabie, his een hard as da shappit flint

we fin near da gyo, whaar a man taks his sye
tae a sea o ryegress, skyims hit as da flicht
o wings. Owreby, a tractor glunshes bales
birls an wips dem, tips dem fae his trapple
inta strings o jet black beads. Some things

bide da sam: rhythms o da aert
da straff o birds apö da banks
an da sea wi her aald skin lirkit.
A reesel o wind, an shades o blue rin
een inta tidder, forivver replenished.

Bio-rhythms

For as long as sea has quarrelled with the land
and fulmers sought a rock ledge in the cliffs
their hoarse cackle has been a homeward hymn
a warning cry. One at sea, one on the nest
each spelling the other: comings and goings mapped
by a black-back, his eye hard as the slither of flint

we find near the *gyo*, where a man takes his scythe
to a sea of ryegrass, skims it as the flight
of wings. Nearby, a tractor gulps down bales
twirls and binds them, tips them from his windpipe
into strings of jet black beads. Some things

stay the same: rhythms of the earth,
the commotion of birds on the cliff edge
and the sea with her old skin creased.
A shiver of wind, and shades of blue run
into one another, forever replenished.

Swans apö Spiggie Loch

Haem in Iceland
whaar mirk o winter
grippit laand, air hüld
a inteemation o snaa.

We felt aert tak da dorts
turn her back ta da sun. We
o snaa pens an icy sinew
wadder lean times.

Tized we wir, soothbye
bi Faroe an Flugga
aye farder, farder, till
we saa Fitful rise.

Quendale is baetin her breest
Scoosburgh battened doon
Spiggie clos stookit. Ness kye
rive hidmost girse.
Dey'll winter in fat byres.

Da loch is a tird o froad.
At da sooth end we lift,
armada afore da wind.
I da lee at da nort end
we feed, neck deep.

Spiggie Loch 'll hoose wis
till aert an sun makk up.
Till dan, we'll grace winter
saaften his bicht. Day lentens
we'll sail nort, spirits o licht.

Swans on Spiggie Loch

Home in Iceland
where winter darkness
gripped land, air held
an intimation of snow.

We felt earth take offence, sulk,
turn her back to the sun. We
of snow flight feathers and icy sinew
weather lean times.

Tempted we were, southwards
by Faroe and Flugga
always further, further, till
we saw Fitful rise.

Quendale is beating her breast
Scoosburgh battened down
Spiggie well harvested. Ness cattle
tear last grass.
They will winter in fat cattle sheds.

The loch is an agitation of froth.
At the south end we lift,
armada before the wind.
In the lee at the north end
we feed, neck deep.

Spiggie Loch will house us
till earth and sun make up.
Till then, we'll grace winter
soften his bight. Day lengthens
we'll sail north, spirits of light.

Paes Eggs

I dy harned haand du hüld ta da licht
een o da eggs at du wid gie her,
morroless laek dee; shaa'd her
hits less dan perfect shaep
da rukkly wye da shall wis med

dat day at du kent whin shö cam
hit wis da hidmost time du'd feel
da lichtness at shö browt. Aa da sam

fur aa da fash o life, da lettin go,
da lettin doon: hit hed ta geng
ee wye or tidder. Da twa ends
owre far apairt ta hadd tagidder

dat day at du pressed
mair as da half dizzen
inta her haands: paes egg
apö paes egg. *Tak care noo.*
Tak twartree mair fur da bairns.

Easter Eggs

In your calloused hand you held to the light
one of the eggs that you would give her,
anomalous like you; showed her
its less than perfect shape
the uneven way the shell was made

that day you knew when she came
it was the last time you would feel
the lightness she brought. All the same

for all the hassle of life, the letting go,
the letting down: it had to go
one way or other. The two ends
too far apart to hold together

that day when you pressed
more than the half dozen
into her hands: Easter egg
upon Easter egg. *Take care now.*
Take a few more for the kids.

Sam but different

Hae'in, fae da start, mair as ee wye o spaekin,
o makkin sense o things, we laern ta fit
whit we say ta whit's lippened. Takk peety apö dem
at's born ta wan tongue: dem at nivver preeve
maet fae idder tables. Raised wi twa languages
is unconscious faestin: twa wyes o tinkin.
Een extends da tidder; can shaa wis anidder wirld
yet foo aa wirlds is jöst da sam, but different.

Same but different

Having, from the start, more than one way of speaking,
of making sense of things, we learn to fit
what we say to what's expected. Take pity on those
born to one tongue: those who never taste even a morsel
from other tables. Raised with two languages
is unconscious feasting: two ways of thinking.
One extends the other; can show us another world
yet how all worlds are just the same, but different.

Yarbent

i m my Aunt Ella

You took time ta mak sure I'd gotten
ivery tirl, ivery whenk o da wird
you'd used: dat een I'd aksed aboot.
Sic a aald wird hit soonded: *yarbent*.

I can still see you luik ta Mousa, say
'Weel, hit's a boo o wadder fae da sooth-aest,
laid on herd an dry, no laek ta shift,
maybe roond voar, or eftir hairst.'

Der a yarbent settled apön me fae you göd:
sic a peerie wird, but nirse. A'll varg
i da face o him, an keep i da mind's eye,
as you wir wint tae, da bigger pictir.

Yarbent

i m my Aunt Ella

You took time to make sure I'd understood
every twist, every odd movement of the word
you'd used: that one I'd asked about.
It sounded such an old word: *yarbent.*

I can still see you look to Mousa, say
'Well, it's a spell of weather from the south-east,
laid on hard and dry, not likely to shift,
maybe round Spring planting, or after harvest.'

There's a *yarbent* settled on me since you died:
such a small word, but bitter. I'll toil
in the face of it, and keep in the mind's eye,
as you used to, the bigger picture.

Chance o a lifetime

for Daniel

Fae da aeroplane, taas o licht pick oot
a peerie toon, plunkit dere bi chance:
a accidence o burns an broos,
heads an tails o nature's providence.

Fur wis, nae mair nae less, da time
an place an fortune o wir birth
is happenstance; dine an mine,
mi jewel, as dicey as da rest.

Hed dis fine braidin o wir burn no come,
– dis blissit odds – I wid a virmished
fur hit. Whin du's aroond, dy fun
an lichtsomeness sends ivery penny dirlin
i da air, ta laand da richt wye up,
heads or tails, whitivver wye is ca'ad.

Chance of a lifetime

for Daniel

From the aeroplane, streaks of light pick out
a little town, plumped down there by chance:
an accidence of streams and slopes,
heads and tails of nature's providence.

For us – no more, no less – the time
and place and fortune of our birth
is happenstance; yours and mine,
my love, as random as the rest.

Had this fine braiding of our stream not come,
– this blessèd odds – I would have pined long
for it. When you're around, your fun
and cheerfulness send every penny spinning
in the air, to land the right way up,
heads or tails, whichever one is called.

Glims o origin

I savoured dy aerly wirds as dey cam,
whinivver dey surprised dy mooth;
helpit shape dem wi dee, hent dem.

Foo mony generations o bairns
is quarried dat sam wirds, fun
aa needfu soonds aroond dem?

An sea-farers at laandit here
höved in, fae uncan erts, wirds
kjerried on ocean's shiftin tides;

wave-wörn, wind-riven wirds,
der aedges shaaved aff, makkin
a meld; a tongue fit fur saga

an fur psalm. Rumse ithin hit,
hock awa, an du'll fin veins
i da steyn, bricht glims o origin!

Glints of origin

I savoured your early words as they came,
whenever they surprised your mouth;
helped shape them with you, gather them.

How many generations of children
have quarried those same words, found
all needful sounds around them?

And sea-farers who landed here
threw in, from unfamiliar places, words
carried on ocean's shifting tides;

wave-worn, wind-riven words,
their edges hacked aff, making
a blend; a tongue fit for saga

and for psalm. Rummage in it,
dig away, and you'll find veins
in the stone, bright glints of origin!

Nae aesy mizzer

A polar projection changes foo we figure oot
wir world. Shetland isna banished tae a box
i da Moray Firt or left oot aa tagidder

– ta scale up da rest – but centre stage.
Peripheral has new meanin; an marginal.
Perspective changes trowe da years: we age,

pit wir trust in aalder maps: imperfect,
but shaain a wirld eence kent. Nae satellites
ta fix a point, nae aesy mizzer, but wi pictirs

decoratin da aedges – da fowr saesons,
da seeven winders o da wirld, da furies,
an weird sea munsters ta gluff a sailor.

Da wye twa bairns, unsure, first stare
at een anidder is foo we size up intention,
map wir territory, laern hit's safe ta share.

See me noo as du wid a aald map: finger
hit lichtly; enjoy hits mizzerlessness,
da marginalia, da element o winder.

No easy measure

A polar projection changes how we figure out
our world. Shetland isn't banished to a box
in the Moray Firth or left out all together

– to scale up the rest – but centre stage.
Peripheral has new meaning; and marginal.
Perspective changes through the years: we age,

put our trust in older maps: imperfect,
but showing a world once known. No satellites
to fix a point, no easy measure, but with pictures

decorating the edges – the four seasons,
the seven wonders of the world, the furies,
and weird sea monsters to frighten a sailor.

The way two children, unsure, first stare
at one another is how we size up intention,
map our territory, learn it's safe to share.

See me now as you would an old map: finger
it lightly; enjoy its measurelessness,
the marginalia, the element of wonder.

Imprint

Whaarivver we ir, der aye someen nort-by.
Only at da pole wid a compass birl, seek
magnetic certainty.

Whaarivver we ir on dis tirlin hemisphere
Polaris tracks wir waavellin. Shö's preened
ta da firmament; a stey.

Whaarivver we ir, nort is a state o mind
wi nae slack: aert's loops taen in,
da tap graftit aff.

Whaarivver we ir, a scanner wid jalouse
wir belangin da wye a stick o rock aans
hits origin.

Whaarivver we ir, slippit laek homin doos,
der a gaet nort. Somethin keeps nyiggin
dat invisible treed.

Imprint

Wherever we are, there's always someone further north.
Only at the Pole would a compass spin, seek
magnetic certainty.

Wherever we are on this turning hemisphere
Polaris tracks our staggering. She's pinned
to the firmament; a prop, a guy.

Wherever we are, north is a state of mind
with no slack: earth's stitches taken in,
the top grafted off.

Wherever we are, a scanner would suspect
our belonging the way a stick of rock reveals
its origin.

Wherever we are, freed like homing pigeons,
there's a path north. Something keeps tugging
that invisible thread.

Catchin da licht

Labradorite

Sailors plied da Nort Atlantic,
der windjammers ballastit
wi steyn taen fae Labrador,
da ebbs o Newfoondland.
Naethin as dour as sea anunder

a skull-kep o clood, mooskit
or shaela. Wind backin, bassel
o weet thwack apö sail,
an da shift o steyns reeselin
i da howld wi ivery rowl.

Naethin sae grey, sae dull
as dis labradorite dey shöled,
naethin sae ösless. But wi taas
o licht, a glink apön hit, an hüld
at da richt angle, whit dey saa

wis da wing o a dragonfly,
hits shiller o blues, glister
o maaves an greens an, fur
da takkin, prisms o simmer:
haem shores, a lift o azure.

I da slack times, wi sails flaagin,
a nort man wid tak a slidder
o steyn, polish an dicht hit,
see hit flaachter on a flan, winder
on bluest een catchin da licht.

Catching the light

Labradorite

Sailors plied the North Atlantic,
their windjammers ballasted
with stone taken from Labrador,
the foreshores of Newfoundland.
Nothing as dismal as sea under

a skull-cap of cloud, mousey-grey
or dark grey. Wind backing, beat
of wet thwack on sail,
and the shift of stones jostling
in the hold with every roll.

Nothing so grey, so dull
as this labradorite they shovelled,
nothing so useless. But with streaks
of sunlight, a gleam on it, and held
at the best angle, what they saw

was the wing of a dragonfly,
its shiller of blues, glitter
of mauves and greens and, for
the taking, prisms of summer:
home shores, a sky of azure.

In slack times, with sails flapping loosely,
a northern man would take a slither
of stone, polish and gently wipe it,
see it flutter on a sudden gust, wonder
about bluest eyes catching the light.

Frakka

Frakka staands at her door. Da daal is
shaltered but lanerly: gaets geng by her.

Da sun can barely glisk her window
but her mödow is fat, her kye stuggit.

Her name maps da burn at her back:
shö sets a trootie-net across hits mooth;

wirks till mirknen: fair-skinned,
soopple i da wind at toosles her hair.

Her strent at da crö is aert-kent:
shö can roo a yowe in a meenit.

Shö luiks tae her sheep apö da heogan,
keeps dem fae Da Trowie Burn.

Dey roam fae Grímr's ferm ta Burra Dale;
een smored i Da Steis til Kaitrin.

Her aald fock keep da fire in,
bairns rin wi a kishie o paets.

Since her man wis lost affa Nesting
een fae Da Kalef helps wi da hairst kill.

Shö lins her at da door, skiles fur whin
his boat 'll roond Da Muckle Ayre.

Micht da voe bring her a new lover?
Shö's wöshen her linen, reddit her hair.

Frakka

Frakkafjeld, Dale – 1000 AD

Frakka stands at her door. The valley is
sheltered but lonely: paths go past her.

The sun can barely glimpse her window
but her meadow is fat, her cattle well fed.

Her name maps the stream at her back:
she sets a net for trout across its mouth;

works till dusk: fair-skinned,
supple in the wind that tousles her hair.

Her strength at the sheep-fold is legendary:
she can strip a fleece off in a minute.

She keeps an eye on her sheep on the common,
keeps them from The Trowie Burn.

They roam from Grímr's farm to Burra Dale;
one drowned in The Steis til Kaitrin.

Her old folk keep the fire in,
children run with a basket of peats.

Since her husband was lost off Nesting
one from The Kalef helps with the harvest kill.

She rests briefly at the door, peers for when
his boat will round The Muckle Ayre.

Might the *voe* bring her a new lover?
She has washed her linen, combed out her hair.

Da sea, hjarta

Da sea's haand trivvels da trimmlin limb
o laand: daily shö wylcomes his comins
an gyaains; der sochs an quwilks aboot
der secret tryst; a rivin an lettin go
athin der makkin o blaahöl or a gyo.
Sometimes he's filsket an höves himsel
far far intil her, till shö's sabbin, plötin.
Lang micht he seek her oot, lang meld

wi her, ta keep her young an vital.
Shö's fairest dere ithin his touch;
her frame buskit wi banks-flooers,
bouquets o aert-bark, violet an squill.
Shö'll age peerie-wyes, lowse his grip
apön her; lippen a mair gentle lover.

The sea, beloved one

The sea's hand explores the trembling limb
of land: daily she welcomes his comings
and goings; there are sighs and swallowings in
their secret tryst; a ripping up and letting go
in their creating a blowhole or a *gyo*.
Sometimes he's high-spirited and heaves himself
far far into her, till she's soaking, pleading.
Long might he seek her out, long become one

with her, to keep her young and vital.
She's fairest there within his touch;
her body decorated with sea-pinks,
bouquets of tormentil, violet and squill.
She'll age gently, loosen his grip
on her; expect a more gentle lover.

Hairst blinks

Een glinder at stoorin sun.
I da lea, simmer's dregs.
Roond a coarner, a trooker
o a nort wind frisks wis. Da lift
blackens, lichtens. Hadd fast
trowe makkin an brakkin,
swidderin time; keep clos
whit you hae: a delusion but

mair real as dis doontöm;
rain staandin affa da aert,
sae drookit you gaff. Geng
halfers wi een anidder.
Bi mirknen da lip o day
trimmels, haert i da mooth.
Share da glöd, as farder
an farder da sun hoids her.

Summer lightning

Eyes narrow at the sun's stare.
In the lea, summer's dregs.
Round a corner, a ruffian
north wind frisks us. The sky
blackens, lightens. Hold fast
through making and breaking,
swithering time; keep close
what you have: a delusion but

more real than this downpour;
rain bouncing off the earth,
so drenched you laugh. Split
the difference with one another.
By twilight the lip of day
trembles, heart in the mouth.
Share the afterglow, as further
and further the sun hides.

Blue een

Mindin on dat blue een
at clappit saaft apö me
an daeved as keenly.

Hit's a blue ceonothus day,
unsure o hitsel. Late frost,
dan sun spierin trowe;

simmer wi a hint, a skröf
o winter. Fock still happit.
A man at da boddom

o a ledder, luiks up. Da lift is
a blue forivver. A dug, twistit
roond apön himsel, clooers

at da scab dat's no laek ta heal.
As I geng I man trust; takk
da blue een wi me.

Blue eyes

Remembering those blue eyes
that stroked me softly
and stunned me as easily.

It's a blue ceonothus day,
unsure of itself. Late frost,
then sun questing through;

summer with a hint, a veneer
of winter. Folk still well wrapped up.
A man at the bottom

of a ladder, looks up. The sky is
a blue forever. A dog, twisted
round upon itself, scratches

at the scab that's unlikely to heal.
As I go I must trust; take
the blue eyes with me.

On da reboond

Dunna tell me dy saga,
A'm seek o narrative;
nor spaek o blue-melts
or foo things dowe:
eemages only geeng sae far.
Cut tae da quick,

tae da heart o hit,
da pluperfect:
ta whaar du's bön;
an whaar – wi da glied een
o mislippenin – du's dippit dee,
whaar du micht geeng.

In a list o wirds
hit lies atween rebuff
an rebirth, near enyoch
ta rebel an rebigg.
Du micht refleck:
defleck echo, re-echo

dan boond back fornenst
soondin-board, setback,
an ivery faas dimriv, inta
da present tense,
da here an noo
o dy new scrievin ...

On the rebound

Don't tell me your saga,
I'm sick of narrative;
nor speak of bruising
or how things fade:
images only go so far.
Cut to the quick,

to the heart of it,
the pluperfect:
to where you've been;
and where – through distorted vision
of rejection – you've sat down,
where you might go.

In a list of words
it lies between rebuff
and rebirth, near enough
to rebel and rebuild.
You might even reflect:
deflect echo, re-echo

then bound back against
sounding-board, setback,
and every false dawn, into
the present tense,
the here and now
of your new writing ...

At sixty

Dat line whaar birds, hurless, cross
a treshel-tree, winter at der back,
or a skirl o simmer afore dem.

Whaar, alang da sixtieth parallel,
sheerlin on ringin strings vimmers
on a nordern palette. Hingin in

ta tree score year is harkin fur dat line,
anidder saison o sang. Hit's pushin
fornenst da door, liftin da sneck, takkin

da fiddle doon an tunin whit's left ta mak
da notes. Fingers rekk farder, trivvel
da missin string, tize oot da melody.

At sixty

That line where birds, exhausted, cross
a threshold, winter at their back,
or a happy intimation of summer before them.

Where, along the sixtieth parallel,
birdsong on resonating strings trembles
on a northern palette. Hanging in

to three score years is listening for that line,
another season of song. It's pushing
against the door, lifting the latch, taking

the fiddle from the wall and tuning what's left to make
the notes. Fingers reach further, gently compensate
for the missing string, draw out the melody.

Love in a caald climate

Hit wisna his widden palin
nor da oppenwark o steyns set
ta brack da wind, nor
da hedder he prammed
atween fences; nor

da tang he tör fae da ebb
an turned an turned, nor
his fingers brakkin clods;
nor wis hit da sun scrimin
peerie-wyes. Na, hit wis

da draem shö plantit
an a rösin ithin her luik
as shö stakit hit, willin
da wan rose ta oppen,
ta hadd mirknen.

Love in a cold climate

It wasn't his wooden paling
nor the lattice of stones set
to break the wind, nor
the heather he packed tightly
between fences; nor

the seaweed he tore from the foreshore
and turned and turned, nor
his fingers breaking clods;
nor was it the sun peering
gently. No, it was

the dream she planted
and a praising in her look
as she staked it, willing
the one rose to open,
to hold the long dusk.

Dat trickster sun

… ee day he fills your window wi shaeps
o laands at you could mak your ain:
islands beyond islands, draemscapes
you could aa but map: a refrain o

licht troo a peen o gless; incongruities,
tizin places you'll nivver win tae.
You're stuck i da here an noo;
der oot o rekk, maist laek infinity.

… ee day he tirls a rainbow deep intil
anidder een. Cringed, dey rin wi you.
You could aa but lay a haand apö dem,
licht troo silence: a holy hubbelskyu,

da foo spectrum o taer-draps; a slow air
ta turn you inside oot, ta brak a haert.

That trickster sun

... one day it fills your window with shapes
of lands that you could make your own:
islands beyond islands, dreamscapes
you could almost map: a refrain of

light through a pane of glass; incongruities,
enticing places you'll never reach.
You're stuck in the here and now;
They are out of range, much like infinity.

... one day it upturns a rainbow deep into
another one. Coupled together, they run with you.
You could almost lay a hand upon them,
light through silence: a holy uproar,

the full spectrum of tear-drops; a slow melody
to turn you inside out, to break a heart.

Discontinuity

I could blame da wye da sea is smoothed
da steyns; da sylk o touch; da waelin, laevin;
an will da haert be dere whin I come back?

Or I could blame da saandiloo. He wis clear
whit wye ta geng: dis wye noo, nae luikin
owre your shooder. Tide dusna wait;

see da wye da swill o joy is drained.
Dance daday. Damoarn you slip
inta eternity.

Or I could blame da hush at fills you
til you're laek ta burst wi aa da wirds
at could be said but you hadd back.

Hit's whit happens whin you step
in time, but sense a fault-line vimmerin
trowe you: dis side or dat?

Only da sea can greet an sing at da sam time:
shade an licht: cobalt, ultramarine an dan
da lönabrak – a tize, a frush o whicht.

Discontinuity

I could blame the way the sea has smoothed
the stones; the silk of touch; the sifting, leaving;
and will the heart be there when I come back?

Or I could blame the ringed plover. He was clear
which way to go: this way now, no looking
over your shoulder. Tide doesn't wait;

see the way the swill of joy has drained.
Dance today. Tomorrow you slip
into eternity.

Or I could blame the silence that fills you
to bursting-point with all the words
that could be said but you hold back.

It's what happens when you step
in time, but sense a fault-line trembling
through you: this side or that?

Only the sea can cry and sing at the same time:
shade and light: cobalt, ultramarine and then
the breaking wave – an enticing froth of white.

Dis material wirld

Iceland's haert is lowin: aald aert spewin her guts up,
flames spunkin fornenst ice, a azin furnace, black ess.

Dis nae mythic cauldron laek i da *Mirknen o da Gods*,
whin fire wis cöst apö da aert, an aathin skomfished;

dan man an wife waakenin tae a laand remade,
wi dew apö da grund an a new mön an a new sun.

Nor is hit apocalyptic inklins: rumours o wars, o starns
burnin laek lamps, o a time whin aathin's gien; tochts

styooched tae da solar winds, weel furt o da rational;
nor a hidmost renderin o *Da Ring*, da Valkyries fleein.

Na, dis jöst aert rearrangin hersel, raamished, unsettled;
mindin wis o her wyes an timelines, wir momentariness.

Ee day, we'll geng; no brunt bi indifferent physics, but
sweed laek new kishies. We micht glink i da firmament,

hent whaar knowledge ends an history shades ta story,
whaar imagination an poetry is jöst da beginnin.

This material world

Iceland's heart is alight: old earth vomiting her guts up,
flames sparking against ice, a blazing furnace, black ash.

This is no mythic cauldron as in the *Twilight of the Gods*,
when fire was cast on the earth and everything overwhelmed;

then man and wife wakening to a land remade,
with dew on the ground and a new moon and a new sun.

Nor is it apocalyptic inklings: rumours of wars, of stars
burning like lamps, of a time when everything's gone; thoughts

as dust to the solar winds, well beyond the rational;
nor a final rendering of *The Ring*, the Valkyries fleeing.

No, this is just earth rearranging herself, unslept, unsettled;
reminding us of her ways and timelines, our momentariness.

One day, we'll go; not incinerated by indifferent physics, but
singed like new *kishies*. We might gleam in the firmament,

glean where knowledge ends and history shades to story,
where imagination and poetry are just the beginning.

Naethin but big flooers

Hit's dat time o year:
winter claes fae da closet.
I mi window, sunflooers is
tellin me somethin idder.

Der vibrant trussit chic –
plaags, kinda dissolute,
hingin affa da shooder,
a wisp o escapin hair.

Van Gogh paintin awa
writin tae his bridder foo
life is short; an even shorter
da bold years ta face aathin.

Fornenst a glöd o blue
haloed i da window
der message is beyond price,
da auctioneer's hammer.

Though a shadow is cöst owre
der sunny faces, resolutely
refusin ta oppen, der gorgeous:
fae foo bloom ta widderin.

Nothing but big flowers

It's that time of year:
winter clothes from the closet.
In my window, sunflowers are
telling me something other.

Their vibrant unkempt chic –
tatters, somewhat dissolute,
hanging off the shoulder,
a wisp of escaping hair.

Van Gogh painting away
writing to his brother how
life is short; and even shorter
the bold years to face everything.

Against a glow of blue
haloed in the window
their message is beyond price,
the auctioneer's hammer.

Though a shadow is cast over
their sunny faces, resolutely
refusing to open, they are gorgeous:
from full bloom to withering.

Inteemation

Hit cam a haet simmer, whin I wis boarn,
eftir a hap o fanns. You telt me dat,

da moarnin eftir, dey wir a cuckoo
i da berry-bush; an nivver een sin syne.

Your haert aye liftit whin you heard
tirricks back apö da skerry, a aerly tjaldur

or a raingös makkin fur da hill. Whin
granny deed, I kent somethin wis up.

Whin your bridders deed, you nearly gret;
nivver liftit your een ta see da birds.

Eftir you were gien, dad's letters wis
foo o da raingös, tirrick, tjaldur.

Daday, a cuckoo soondit troo da dimriv.
Whitna unreffellin i da unlippened soond.

Intimation

It came a hot summer, when I was born,
after a shawl of deep snow. You told me that,

the morning after, there was a cuckoo
in the berry-bush; and never one since then.

Your heart always lifted when you heard
arctic terns back on the skerry, an early oyster catcher

or a red-throated diver on its way to the hill. When
granny died, I knew something was wrong.

When your brothers died, you nearly wept;
never lifted your eyes to see the birds.

After you had died, dad's letters were
full of the diver, tern, oyster catcher.

Today, a cuckoo sounded through the dawn.
What an unravelling in the unexpected sound.

A meditation apön takkin wir time

Dis very meenit, *noo*, is smootit aff
ithin time's physics. Hit stricks wis,
but's gien afore da mind is taen hit in.

Dis teeterin apön da very aedge o life,
o love; barely braethin in case a Mad Hatter
comes loupin at you, burdeened wi
lost opportunities, missed appointments.

Da hidmist tirrick is fledged, peerie-wyes.
Here ee meenit, gien da neist; left ta fin
his ain wye sooth, ta tiev anidder simmer.

Afore aathin slips inta da past tense o hairst,
I watch dry girse riffle i da stank an dockens
tipper stiff apö der *pointes*. Scabious staands
prood, a maave defiance stabbin da retina

in his ain time. Daylicht's shorter, but
da sun's still haddin. Da mantra man be 'noo',
while we touch a mintie inklin o da present.

A'm resettin da clock: bendin time, mizzerin hit
bi da slow sab o watter trowe floss, da niff o moor.
Low sun is writin aa da peerie wirlds o da hill
an da vod croft is a fine-textured Book o Ooers.

A meditation on taking our time

This very minute, *now*, has slunk off
within time's physics. It strikes us,
but has gone before the mind has clocked it.

This teetering on the very edge of life,
of love; barely breathing in case a Mad Hatter
comes leaping at you, burdened with
lost opportunities, missed appointments.

The final arctic tern has fledged, slowly.
Here one minute, gone the next; left to find
its own way south, to steal another summer.

Before everything slips into the past tense of autumn,
I watch dry grass riffle in the ditch and docks
poised stiffly on their tiptoes. Scabious stands
exposed, a mauve defiance stabbing the retina

in its own time. Daylight is shorter, but
the sun is still holding on. The mantra must be 'now',
while we touch the tiniest inkling of the present.

I'm resetting the clock: bending time, measuring it
by the slow soak of water through rushes, the smell of moor.
Low sun is writing all the little worlds of the hill
and the abandoned croft is a fine-textured Book of Hours.

'If only a steyn could spaek'

after Norman MacCaig

Days followed nichts o tömald, an a puddock cruggit
anunder da dimaloorie lean-tö o wir doormat;
a squatter, his spottit skyin silky as da steyn
du slippit inta mi haand. Hits spots wis
laek een, du said.

      Hit wis slicht as da ebb
steyns o dat abacus mi faider biggit, peerie-wyes,
coontin da years, dellin wi da döl
o da day, luikin nedder ahint, nor ahead:
a meenit o balance, kinda bairnly-laek;

      an as wörn as
da steyns mi son biggit, decades later – beach boy,
beach man: tree pebbles, aa waeled wi care;
placed, adjustit, dan keppit wi a flat steyn;
da pattren repeatit, willin hit upward,
taperin tae da tap; a antrin wavvel.

      Foo a steyn
can lowse da tongue, wird an sang-bricht.
Whitna a fine cabbi-labbi da sea spawns,
een foo o questions ta live, dis meenit's tale;
laek da puddock, waitin fur da rain ta white, ta escape
his lodgin. I clesp da steyn less hit loups
fae mi surprised haand.

'If only a stone could speak'

after Norman MacCaig

Days followed nights of rain, and a frog skulked
under the dismal lean-to of our doormat;
a squatter, his spotted skin silken as the stone
you slipped into my hand. Its spots were
like eyes, you said.

        It was smooth as the beach
stones of that abacus my father built, slowly,
counting the years, dealing with the sadness
of the day, looking neither behind, nor ahead:
a moment of balance, oddly playful;

        and as worn as
the stones my son built, decades later – beach boy,
beach man: three pebbles, each picked with care;
placed, adjusted, then capped with a flat stone;
the pattern repeated, willing it upward,
tapering to the top; an occasional wobble.

        How a stone
can loosen the tongue, word and song-bright.
What animated conversation the sea spawns,
eyes full of questions to live, this moment's story;
like the frog, waiting for the rain to stop, to escape
his lodging. I clasp the stone in case it leaps
from my surprised hand.

Whit's in a name?

If and whin A'm foryat mi name
and gaan at dee laek a doitin sowl

lat me spend a day parked bi Suilven,
stumpsed bi jap o watter. Turn

mi calendar bi da laekly o da hills
an set mi watch bi shadows pö da loch.

Forgie me if I canna mind fur why we cam
or mi gaze cloods in a cod-fysh kind o wye

or if da name I gied ta dee is mizzled aff.
A'll still feel mountain, watter, love.

What's in a name?

If and when I have mislaid my name
and stare at you disconcertingly

let me spend a day parked by Suilven,
perplexed by broken water. Turn

my calendar to the mountain's season,
and set my watch by shadows on the loch.

Forgive me if I lose the reason that we came
or my gaze clouds in a cod-fish kind of way

or if the name I chose for you eludes me.
I'll still sense mountain, water, love.

Conundrums

Da Grind o da Navir, Aeshaness

At da café, someen tried a puzzle med o wid,
a ticht knot. Takkin apairt wis aesy; piece
bi piece, no bafft an brukkit tae a coose. Pitten

tagidder took mair as patience. Hit's da story
o wir lives: fittin in wi een anidder, readin
da pattren, steppin peerie wyes. But, my gori,

whittan a backdrap! Da Heads o Grokken,
Da Drongs: ootmarkers o fechts an spöllis.
Da ocean here is wild, weel wint wi takkin

gyoppmfoos; he's riven hit sindry, tirled
hulters headicraa, höved dem dis wye an dat.
Maybe, in a tirse, he birsed da watter intil

a cave whaar da basalt, brokkin inta blocks,
offert her waekness. He balled his seevent wave
at her sindered boady, sang as he shockit her,

dan poored his proil owre her; an a pöl, sae shö
could see her puzzled face fornenst his. If you hae
da haert, poo oot da keystane, gie yoursel up.

Conundrums

Da Grind o da Navir, Aeshaness

At the café, someone tried a puzzle made of wood,
a tight knot. Taking apart was easy; piece
by piece, neither a struggle nor a demolition. Putting it

together took more than patience. It's the story
of our lives: fitting in with one another, reading
the pattern, stepping gently. But, Good God,

what a backdrop! The Heads of Grokken,
The Drongs: outmarkers of fights, of bashing and breaking.
The ocean here is wild, accustomed to taking

double handfuls; he has riven it apart, made
huge rocks do somersaults, heaved them this way and that.
Maybe, in high spirits, he squeezed the water into

a cave where the basalt, broken into blocks,
offered her weakness. He threw his seventh wave
at her sundered body, sung as he choked her,

then poured his stolen hoard over her; and a pool, so she
could see her puzzled face against his. If you have
the heart, pull out the keystone, give yourself up.

Beach wark

Fedaland

We nedder spleet nor weighed da tusk, da ling,
nor laid dem oot ta dry; but played wis apö da beach,
left a steepel o steyns fur da ocean.

We nivver shoardit da sixern – kept her lyin aff
i wir memory; set wis i da bosie o her noost,
shared wir faerdie-maet.

We nedder cut nor cured a paet, nor gaddered
wrack; but windered on haertsteyns,
fires ithin simmer böds.

Nae wirds spokken, nane needed.
Du waeled me twa boannie steyns
an walkit ahint me.

Beach work

Fedaland

We neither split nor weighed the cod, the ling,
nor laid them out to dry; but played upon the beach,
left a pyramid of stones for the ocean.

We didn't prop up the yoal – kept her lying off
in our memory; sat down in the bosom of her *noost*,
shared our food for the journey.

We neither cut nor cured a peat, nor gathered
driftwood; but wondered about hearthstones,
fires within summer bothies.

Few words were spoken, none were needed.
You selected for me two pretty stones
and walked behind me.

Soondscapes

I da dizzied hoose, a strum o flees baet
endless drums fornenst a frenzied window.
Belligerent, dey want nedder in nor oot.

Apö da broo, ahint a wheeshtit chapel,
twa windmills spin new soondscapes owre
da laand, kert-wheelin alleluias.

I da cloistert granite der a orchestration
o birds, a oorie whirr, a vimmerin
o whaaps an peewits. Da wind

troo da grind is a spaekin in tongues
wi da bruckit feed-hoop tunin in:
idder-wirldly, intimately insistent.

Aa dis music ta lö tae, ta slip inta:
a aald organ nönin, a hushie hubbelskyu.
Up owre da hill, airms turn, da haert lifts.

Soundscapes

In the dizzied house, a strum of blue-bottles beat
endless drums against a frenzied window.
Belligerent, they want neither in nor out.

On the hill-brow, behind a silent chapel,
two windmills spin new soundscapes over
the land, cart-wheeling alleluias.

In the cloistered granite there is an orchestration
of birds, an eerie whirr, a quiver
of curlew and lapwing. The wind

through the gate is a speaking in tongues
with the broken feed-hoop tuning in:
other-worldly, intimately insistent.

All this music to listen to intently, to slip into:
an old organ droning, an uproarious lullaby.
Up over the hill, arms turn, the heart lifts.

Ivery day, reboarn

Rönas Voe

Wir prammed ithin kayaks, peerie waavellin
wirlds, tensed tae da ocean. Canyoned abön,
Rönas Hill slips by, haddin her böried haert:
red granite aawye, slow revelation fae da dark.

Ice is steepened her face, da sea roughed her up.
Daday, i da cleft o her voe, Atlantic masons
salist; but hammer an chisel still at da ready
ta taper a pillar, sklent a stack, cloor oot a cave.

Is hit a game der set fur wis, ta waeve atween,
dodge danger? Watter swittles an swinkles,
slaps affa da side o da craft, tilts her;
wir sense o depth is in a snurl: hit's laek

wearin someen idder's glesses. We mak on
wir wint wi aeons, ken whaar wir gyaain,
can defy danger. Wir seen shappit baas afore,
taen risks. But dis is laernin ta see things

a different wye. We scrimp trowe dark cracks
inta da licht, lugs tuned tae da snush
an snyirk o da sea, da lap, da gentle clap.
Lie back, hadd in your paddle, pass trowe

da eye o da needle, nug trowe da dark trenkie,
kyistit, while da tide's low, while der a meenit.
Look deep time i da eye, shaa hit faerlessness
as hit comes in apön you, aa but trottles you.

Dig in, poo troo, keep her trim; come oot
da tidder side, inta da blue, smilin.

Every day, reborn

Rönas Voe

We're crammed in kayaks, tiny wobbling
worlds, tensed to the ocean. Canyoned above,
Rönas Hill slips by, holding her entombed heart:
red granite all the way, slow revelation from the dark.

Ice has steepened her face, the sea roughed her up.
Today, in the cleft of her *voe*, Atlantic masons
take a break; but hammer and chisel still at the ready
to taper a pillar, slice a stack, claw out a cave.

Is this a game they've set for us, to weave between,
dodge danger? Water splashes gently and swallows,
slaps off the side of the craft, tilts her;
our sense of depth is distorted: it's like

wearing someone else's glasses. We pretend
we're familiar with aeons, know where we're going,
can defy danger. We've seen submerged reefs before,
taken risks. But this is learning to see things

a different way. We scrimp through dark cracks
into the light, ears tuned to the sniffy snort
and creaky sounds of the sea, the lap, the gentle stroke.
Lie back, hold in your paddle, pass through

the eye of the needle, nudge through the dark passageway,
coffined, while the tide is low, while there's a moment.
Look deep time in the eye, show it fearlessness
as it comes in on you, almost throttles you.

Dig in, pull through, keep her trim; come out
the other side, into the blue, smiling.

Dis life is nivver enyoch

1
'Kuml' – Pagan burial site
(Iceland National Museum)

Shö lies, foetal, in a shell-saand grave
apön her richt side, maybe facin da sun;
twa steyns abön her skull
een at her fit.

Her left hench-bane lies across her richt
da knap-bane below da tidder een
left airm curled inta her richt airm.
Shaklebanes, fingers, cöts, taes
der aa dere, young an unwörn.

Her grave-goods: twa shalls,
a pebble, whit micht a bön a blade.
Naethin ta busk her fur her journey
nedder beads nor redder;
an nae sign o a lover.
Best no tink o her final ooers
fur der a peerie grave aside her
wi a rikkel o mintie banes.
Twa steyns at da head, een at da fit.

***

I lie i mi bed on mi richt side, foetal,
facin aest. Mi left knee rests jöst below
da tidder, left airm across mi bosie.
A'm said mi göd wirds, an tanks
fur tree score year an ten.
But I still draem laek a pagan.

2
Christian burial (1916-1918)
(Hólavallagarður Cemetery, Reykjavik)

Fowr fine sons lie here:
tree deed young, barely twa year
apairt. Wha kens what ailed dem?
Did da Great Frost Winter tak hits toll?

Der böried tagidder, sidey-fur-sidey,
da grave aest-wast. Laid oot straicht,
apö der backs, haands likkly crossed.
Only Stefán med hit ta fifty, maybe
outlived da midder an faider.
Murnin claes wis nivver affa da back,
blinnds barely liftit.

But noo hit's a gairden, a Eden,
wi whitebeam an rowan
an birds i der thoosands
brakkin da silence.

***

Whin I win haem I email mi son,
tell him da birds wis a chorus,
dey jöst aboot daeved me;
an da bunches o berries on rowans
wis redder as blöd.

3
Eftir Etgar Keret, Israeli writer

Da peerie bairn akses da faider
Foo lang do fock live fur?
Da faider says
Twa hunder year if you dunna smok
Da bairn says

Dat's *no lang enoych*
Da faider cöllies aboot him:
Ya, dat hit is; hit's plenty lang
Da bairn gowls
Na, hit's no nearly lang enoych
Da faider greets wi him
Du's richt, mi jewel.
Hit's no nearly lang enoych.

This life is never enough

1
'Kuml' – Pagan burial site
(Iceland National Museum)

She lies, foetal, in a shell-sand grave
on her right side, maybe facing the sun;
two stones above her skull
one at her feet.

Her left hip-bone lies across her right
the knee-bone below the other one
left arm curled into her right arm.
Wrist-bones, fingers, ankles, toes
they're all there, young and unworn.

Her grave-goods: two shells,
a pebble, what might have been a blade.
Nothing to adorn her for her journey
neither beads nor comb;
and no sign of a lover.
Best not think of her final hours
for there's a little grave beside her
with a shrunken heap of tiny bones.
Two stones at the head, one at the foot.

***

I lie in mi bed on my right side, foetal,
facing east. My left knee rests just below
the other, left arm across my bosom.
I've said my prayers, and thanks
for three score years and ten.
But I still dream like a pagan.

2
Christian burial (1916-1918)
(Hólavallagarður Cemetery, Reykjavik)

Four fine sons lie here:
three died young, barely two years
apart. Who knows what ailment they had?
Did the Great Frost Winter take its toll?

They are buried together, side by side,
the grave east-west. Laid out straight,
on their backs, hands likely crossed.
Only Stefán made it to fifty, maybe
outlived the father and mother.
Mourning garments were interminable,
blinds barely lifted.

But now it's a garden, an Eden,
with whitebeam and rowan
and birds in their thousands
breaking the silence.

***

When I get home I email my son,
tell him the birds were a chorus,
they all but deafened me;
and the bunches of berries on rowans
were redder than blood.

3
After Etgar Keret, Israeli writer

The little child asks the father
How long do people live?
The father says
Two hundred years if you don't smoke
The child says

90 |

That's not long enough
The father consoles him:
Yes, indeed it is; it's quite long enough
The child sobs
No, it's not nearly long enough
The father cries with him
You're right, my dear.
It's not nearly long enough.

Notes

gyo   rocky inlet, most typically short and narrow

kishie   cane or straw basket, shaped for the carrying on the back

morroless   one of a pair, the other missing

noost   a hollowed-out area, above the tideline, where boats were hauled up and kept safe, especially during winter

runnicks   trench drains in a byre

sixern   undecked, six-oared wooden boat

trivvel   grope gently

voe   long inlet, most typically like a mini-fiord

Lizzie Coutts' Knowe (page 20)
da fud/Da Fud: local name given to the flat land at the foot of the slope down to the shore in Waas.

Da cockle shall (page 22)
A traditional intricate lace knitting pattern in which the tip of the shell is made by knitting 13 stitches together

Starn sign (page 26)
My aunt was born on the night World War I started, a night when a comet was seen over Shetland, as reputedly on the night of the birth of Julius Caesar. (Her brothers used to tease her with reference to excerpts from Shakespeare's 'Julius Caesar', Act 2, Scene 2.)

Frakka (page 48)
Frakka was possibly a woman with Norse connections who gave her name to a farm near Lerwick, Shetland. The poem is set c 1000 AD. The place names are still redolent of these earlier times.

Frakkafjeld	*Frakka's hill (now Frakkafield)*
Da Trowie Burn	*The Stream of the Trolls*
Grímr's ferm	*The farm of Grímr (now Gremista)*
Burra Dale	*Valley of the rushes*

Da Steis til Katrin	*Katrin's Stream*
Da Kalef	*Promentory (now Califf)*
Da Muckle Ayre	*The big sand spit*

Naethin but big flooers (page 68)
The poem, including the title, refers to letters Vincent Van Gogh wrote to his brother Theo in August 1888

Whit's in a name? (page 76)
Suilven is a sugar-loaf mountain in the NW Highlands of Scotland

Conundrums (page 78)
Da Grind o da Navir, Aeshaness is an area of cataclysmic rock fall

Beach wark (page 80)
Fedaland is the site of an old remote fishing station, with ruins of fishermen's bothies. Cod were split, salted and dried on the stony beaches, and piled into 'steeples' (pyramids) prior to export.

Acknowledgements

I am deeply indebted to the many people, friends and family, who have encouraged my writing over the years, in the UK and further afield, and to the following publishers of collections from which these poems are drawn:

The Shetland Library
Voes & Sounds (1995)
Wast wi da Valkyries (1997)
Plain Song (2002)

Luath Press
Parallel Worlds (2005)
North End of Eden (2010)

Mariscat Press
Dat Trickster Sun (2014)

Ura Forlag
Glimt av opphav – Glims o Origin (Volda, 2017)

Uncollected poems: grateful thanks to *Gutter* magazine and *The New Shetlander*.

Thanks especially to Laureen Johnson for her generous Foreword and Patricia Borlenghi of Patrician Press for her interest and for her willingness and determination to publish this bilingual volume.